I0418416

Live By Faith

by
Lacey Whittaker & Brenda Shiner

Edited by Lil Barcaski and Linda Hinkle

Published by: GWN Publishing

www.GWNPublishing.com

Cover Design: Kristina Conatser Captured by KC Design

ISBN: 979-8-9863922-2-6

Dedication

This book is for all those crazy faith filled people. They are rare and hard to find. They thrive on that Noah kind of Faith.

ABOUT THIS
Book

Faith that outweighs all doubt. Love that explodes with Praise. A yearning for gracious and generous hearts to all be one in Christ. To be an encourager. To dream and believe all the good things our Father wants to give us. To have hope and never to give up.

There is nothing like Your love, Jesus. Nothing we have ever felt before. Nothing like Your precious overwhelming love. It's a never-ending love. Nothing could stop this love. Nothing. It's a love in full joy. We thank You for this overwhelming love You give. We thank You. It's the only way we could live.

"And it shall come to pass afterward That I will pour out My Spirit on all flesh; Your sons and your daughters shall prophesy, Your old men shall dream dreams, Your young men shall see visions."

Joel 2:28 NKJV

Oh, He has given us all these great things. Just believe. It's not weird, the world makes it weird. Ask for these gifts to prophesy and never miss the opportunity to share His heart with you. Ask for the dreams as keys to unlock the unseen. Ask for visions to see more clear. Ask, oh ask, our Father hears.

Father, Son, Holy Spirit, we acknowledge You. Abba Father, I love You. Thank You for Your Son. Holy Spirit thank You for the power and the gifts. We simply cannot live without them. We need You every day. Every single day we need You. Thank You for sending Your son at all costs. We have been bought, and now we can live loving and knowing this.

Yield. Submit. Kneel down low on bended knee. Honor our Prince of peace. Bow lowly in awe. Bow there in praise. Bow there in faith. Bow there one day. We will see You holy on the throne of grace.

"that at the name of Jesus every knee should bow, of those in heaven, and of those on earth, and of those under the earth,"

Philippians 2:10 NKJV

What's your core? What's your being? Do you have a solid foundation and keep singing when the going gets tough? Is Jesus your core, your everything? Is He the song you declare to sing? Is He deep, deep, deep within? Does the Holy Spirit live? What's your core? Does it pour out love, and hope, and truth? Does it pour out a Father that loves and shines on you? What's your core?

Fill it up with the everlasting goodness He chooses to give us.

"And I will pray the Father, and He will give you another Helper, that He may abide with you forever—"

John 14:16 NKJV

Thank you Father for our helper, our friend, our intercessor. Holy Spirit You are welcome here. Live and breathe a fresh wind inside of me. Take me to new heights. Guide me in the will of my Father. The road less traveled. The path I should be taking. Holy Spirit You are welcome here. Flood me with Your presence every second of every day. This I will choose to hear.

Two, You in me. A pair, a pair, a pair, you see. Two, You in me. What greater way to achieve. Two, two, two a pair. Two, two, two, You hold our cares You push us along, the only two that could be so strong. Two, two, two, I long to be two walking with You.

Jesus, You left us the Holy Spirit. You left us the best. The friend, the confident encourager, the truth, the relationship that chooses You.

You left us, but one day You will be back to take us to heaven that's all we ask. To know You will, to know You have shown. That's how we will move along, by Your Holy Spirit making us strong.

"And this is no empty hope, for God Himself is the one who has prepared us for this wonderful destiny. And to confirm this promise, He has given us the Holy Spirit, like an engagement ring, as a guarantee."

2 Corinthians 5:5 TPT

Three in one, three in one, three in one, Father, the Holy Ghost, and son; three in one. So simple but deep, three in one, I choose to seek. Three in one, the power You hold, three in one, it's all I know. Three in one, You are everything, three in one, it's how I can believe.

Are you speaking life or death? Choose to speak life. Live from the spirit of truth. That great holy pleasing vine. Kill the flesh that causes death.

Never let a bad word come from your lips, but always be clean speaking from repentance.

"It is the Spirit who gives life; the flesh profits nothing. The words that I speak to you are spirit, and they are life."

John 6:63 NKJV

Lord, You shower us with blessings daily. You shower us daily. How could we go a whole day and not grab them? How could we not grab what you intended for thee? How could we miss?

Never let us miss these blessings you shower. Never let us miss how good You are to us. Never let us miss these blessings, Lord, never let us go a day without seeing these blessings Lord, never.

Intimacy. Closeness. Familiar. Friend. All these things Jesus asks of us. How many times do we run from Him? How many times do we choose less than? How many times has He been waiting for you? Choose this intimate relationship and not lose. This is a special gift we all can have. Most take it for granted and never turn back. They never go back to sit with Him. They always keep running without repent.

"Here's the one thing I crave from Yahweh, the one thing I seek above all else: I want to live with Him every moment in His house, beholding the marvelous beauty of Yahweh, filled with awe, delighting in His glory and grace. I want to contemplate in His temple."

Psalms 27:4 TPT

Father, when I pray, I give You my requests, my wills, my heart, I give this all to You knowing You will answer. I give You everything in prayer, knowing and believing You will come through.

Help me fully receive Your ways are higher and know Your timing is mightier than what I may ask. Help me believe help me ask.

"And sow fields and plant vineyards,
That they may yield a fruitful
harvest."

Psalms 107:37 NKJV

Sow and reap. Sow, sow all good things, and in return a beautiful harvest season will be yours. Sow and reap peace and it will be an abundant overflow of praise and thanksgiving.

Sow, sow, sow and reap. Sow and reap.

Abba, I belong to You.

Abba, Abba, Abba, I cherish You.

I hold You close Abba.

I see Your face, Abba.

I hear You call my name Abba.

I cry out, Abba come.

Abba, I need You.

Abba You are my true treasure.

Abba, I worship You.

Abba You are You.

Every day I run to the lover of my soul, as I know this is where I truly ought to lie, living in the presence that has caused me to never die. I'm alive and well and full of joy when I run, run, run to the one.

"Deep within me are these lovesick longings, desires, and daydreams of living in union with You. When I'm near You, my heart and my soul will sing and worship with my joyful songs of You, my true source and spring of life!"

Psalms 84:2 TPT

Be encouraged to be different. To look different. To be laughed at because you have that faith that is crazy. That's the faith that mountains are moved on. That's the faith it took for Noah to look like a complete fool. How about Abraham and Sarah expecting a child at her age? Have the faith the Lord can do anything, then watch Him do it. Make believers out of non-believers. Choose to be the few that live like they have nothing to lose. Have faith that outweighs any doubt or disbelief. Have faith and dream today.

"Honor the Lord with your possessions, And with the firstfruits of all your increase;"

Proverbs 3:9 NKJV

Do you honor Him with everything? Your money, your children, your marriage, everything? Do you believe everything is really His and He gives us gifts? He provides. Do you believe this, or do you strive to acquire all these things with selfish desires?

Give all your possessions to Him. Give Him your children. Give Him your 10 percent and watch how He takes these things and multiplies them.

The faith Mary, the mother of Jesus, had. The faith to know and never look back. The faith it took to endure all she had. The life she gave so Jesus would have. The virgin wife that now had a son. The loving husband that never went wrong. Oh, Mary, how did you have the faith to say yes to our Savior that day? I long to have that kind of faith.

Amen. Amen. Agreed and very well. Yes, and amen. Amen, we agree. Amen with the words You speak. Amen amen. Your will amen. Living for the end, Amen.

"Blessed be the Lord forevermore!
Amen and Amen."

Psalms 89:52 NKJV

Holy, holy, holy are You, Lord. Holy, holy You are so so holy. You are so true. I am so in love with You. Holy, holy, holy, and sure, holy and pure. Keep our eyes holy and set on You. Keep us holy living this life we endure. Holy, holy, holy, I keep because holy, holy, holy is what you seek.

"So, the Lord said, "If you have faith
as a mustard seed, you can say to
this mulberry tree, 'Be pulled up by
the roots and be planted in the sea,'
and it would obey you."

Luke 17:6 NKJV

Do you have this mustard seed kind of faith? Do you really believe if you say to the mulberry tree, be pulled up by the roots and be planted in the sea it would obey your command?

He gives us this power and authority when we believe. He gives us all these greater things when we choose to walk with thee.

Have the faith child, have the faith.

It changes everything.

Jesus, Jesus, Jesus, I love to say Your precious name. Jesus, Jesus, Jesus, all has become. All has become from Your word spoke, all has come without curse. Without division, You came to choose life, You came to choose truth. Jesus, Jesus, Jesus, may that precious name be praised, may that precious name be praised all my days.

Plead the blood of Jesus over your family, your mind, and body. Plead the blood of Jesus. It's your protection. It's your salvation. The blood of Jesus was bought, a high price was paid. Plead it today. Have peace and grace.

"elect according to the foreknowledge of God the Father, in sanctification of the Spirit, for obedience and sprinkling of the blood of Jesus Christ: Grace to you and peace be multiplied."

1 Peter 1:2 NKJV

Your mercy and kindness shall follow us all the days of our life. You have promised these good things to those who believe. You have promised these good things never let it be stolen, the gift of love You have chosen. Yes, mercy and goodness follow us all our days as we sing Your great name in praise.

What's your passion and desire? Is it to see sick ones healed? What about demons casted out?

We hold the power by the Holy Spirit running through us to do these miraculous wonders! Believe it today! You can lay hands on the sick and ask them to be healed in Jesus' name! You can cast out devils by the sound of His praise! You can! Believe this today! You can, He gives us authority and power to reign!

"and to have power to heal sicknesses and to cast out demons:"

Mark 3:15 NKJV

Have joy in encouraging one another along on their journey. Have joy, have pure, everlasting joy, encouraging others along their path, His plan.

When we go through trials, have joy in encouraging to persevere, be strong, be one, and go along encouraging in joy. Joy is a strength He has given.

Have joy encourage to keep on living.

Glory upon glory, upon glory, upon glory, upon glory, upon glory, upon glory, upon glory, upon glory, upon glory, our eyes will never have seen such glory as when we see Thee.

"For You are our glory and joy."

1 Thessalonians 2:20 NKJV

Wake up, wake up, the time is now. Don't live another moment apart from Him. Don't live another day wishing. Live today, the time is now, live for Him you never know when your time is up. Live today for Him. Pour from His cup. Never look back. Live today, all while being glad.

"May He grant you according to your heart's desire, And fulfill all your purpose."

Psalms 20:4 NKJV

What may be your hearts desires? What lies deep in your heart? What do you desire most in life? Do you desire Jesus and His will? Do you desire more than just being still, are you stagnant in faith?

Look deep at your heart's desires in a whole new way. Does it take faith?

Yes.

Does it take obedience and love?

Yes.

Are you hoping one day these desires will be fulfilled? If you walk in His will, He will show you the desires of your heart in a new way. He will show you, and give them; that's our faith.

What does faith look like to you? How does it compare to truth?

Faith is the substance of things unseen. First, oh first, you must believe. Plant that seed deep within. Watch it grow, water it too.

Sow and reap the gift of faith and watch how the Lord pours it out in His overflow of grace.

Your loved poured out we simply cannot grasp. We cannot grasp this love, this overflow, this precious love we would have never known if You didn't come save us. If You didn't choose us.

Thank You for this outpouring of love shown. Thank You, Father, I truly know.

"Lord, keep pouring out Your unfailing love on those who are near You. Release more of Your blessings to those who are loyal to You."

Psalms 36:10 TPT

Do you complain? Do you dread? How long do you simply stay in defeat and displease? How long does it take, days or weeks?

One thing I have found, and I know is true, the longer I wallow, the more pity follows too. So, choose today to drop it all.

Choose today to smile and not fall. Choose today to let go real quick. This will be the greatest way to get back with Him.

Smile.

Live heaven on Earth. You can. Long to live heaven on earth. Could you imagine if we all set out to live this way? If we all broke down our carnal ways. Could you imagine this place if everyone sees with eyes for eternity?

Ask Him. Ask Him today. Ask Father, please, may I see as You see in a whole new way?

"Your kingdom come. Your will be done On earth as it is in heaven."

Matthew 6:10 NKJV

Be an encourager.

There are enough critics, doubters, and haters out there. Choose to encourage. Spread it everywhere. Boost those weary spirits and help those in need. God sent encouragers for you to succeed. Be one, bless one, help one, today. Encouragement is a seed that never loses faith.

"You shall have no other gods before Me."

Exodus 20:3 NKJV

Love your God with all your heart, all your mind, and all your soul. Love Him with everything in you. Love Him first and foremost.

I believe in God the Father, the Son and the Holy Spirit. I believe. I believe. I believe the power You hold. I believe You always know. I believe with great faith. I believe those mighty winds obey.

I believe everything you gave. I believe in that everlasting life one day. I believe You never will change. Oh, I believe. I believe this all my days.

Faith. What stirs our faith? What makes us yearn for that crazy kind of faith?

The spirit stirred up rising above reasoning. The spirit that breaks free. The spirit that truly believes in a God that conquered everything. Keep your faith. Grow your faith. It's your faith that takes you to new reigns. New positions. New things. It's your faith, it's your everything.

Ask in faith.

"But let him ask in faith, with no doubting, for he who doubts is like a wave of the sea driven and tossed by the wind."

James 1:6 NKJV

Be about our Father's business. What does that really mean? It means to put Him first. Love the worst. Forgive and be forgiven. Live and keep on giving. Never look back in the past.

Keep walking forward and always ask. Your will, Father, be done. Thy kingdom come, on earth as it is in heaven. That's the treasure I hold. It's heaven.

Sacrifice. Surrender. Give. Are you selfish or in defeat? Do you think highly of yourself and forget God supplies all your needs? Do you sacrifice or always stay in content? Do you give until it hurts or barely tithe? Do you surrender your pride for His will and life? Do you, oh, do you even know the cost of sacrifice?

"I beseech you therefore, brethren, by the mercies of God, that you present your bodies a living sacrifice, holy, acceptable to God, which is your reasonable service."

Romans 12:1 NKJV

Do you love God more than yourself? Is it Him you would give it all up for? Do you lie down and bow before your Lord? Do you arise and sing His praise? Do you go hours praying for His way? Where does He fall on your priority list?

Make Him first, oh, choose to love Him.

If you really want to live by faith, you cannot walk by sight. It's not possible. It's not possible to really live by faith if you are only wanting to see with your eyes. It's not possible.

You must believe in the unseen! You must be intent in your belief. You must dig deep and know like you know!

Live by this faith He has called us to, you will never regret it, it's true.

"For we walk by faith, not by sight."

II Corinthians 5:7 NKJV

Dying to my flesh daily. I only want to be with You, sit with You, hear You. I long to forever be with You. I die to my flesh so

I can live sitting having communion with You. All my days, I choose to lose myself to live with You. All my days, this is my heart, it's true.

We are all one but what does that mean to you? Living as one is not easy to do. You see how the enemy loves to conflict and divide. You see how he does it with all his lies. Conquer and divide he loves to do, but God sent His son to save us so, why can't we love too?

"Do we not all have one Father? Has not one God created us? Why do we deal treacherously with one another, profaning the covenant of our fathers [with God]?"

Malachi 2:10 AMP

What does it mean to dream? Really dream? Like the dreams that are unreal and out of this world?

Well, it starts by faith.

Having faith like Noah. Believing and trusting that the Lord will do what He says, and His promises always come true. Dream big, then reach a little higher for those dreams that don't make any sense. You will be glad you did.

"Take delight in the Lord, and He will give you your heart's desires."

Psalms 37:4 NLT

Delight, delight, delight in Him. He will fill you up and give you the desires of your heart.

Do you have an encourager in your life? Are you the encouraging one? Do people come to you for a pick me up?

I would say everyone needs at least one in their tribe to survive. To battle, to win, to always get up and try again.

If you don't have one, be one, and pray for one to come. It's the greatest gift given to anyone.

Where does your help come from? A sister, a daughter, a son? Where does your help come from when you are at your low of lows? What if you just need a small push or a heavy tow? Who do you call? Who do you run to?

I can tell you it's easy to run to the ones of this world. Oh, but we have a Father that hears us all. We have a Father that takes us on at all costs. We have a Father. We have a best friend. Why, oh why, is it so hard to choose Him? To choose Him first. Call on Him today He will help in every way!

"*My help comes from the Lord, Who made heaven and earth.*"

Psalms 121:2 NKJV

Obey. Be quick to repent. Obey, be quick to let go. Obey, forgive, and forgive again. Obey, that's what keeps you from going astray.

Do you believe there is only one way?

He is the way. He is the truth. He is life. He is the only way. Jesus is the only way.

Don't waste another day. Go out and preach that the kingdom of heaven is at hand. Go out there, show in love. You

may be the only one that person sees.
That one person has. Jesus left the 99 to
go after that one. Will you?

"Jesus said to him, "I am the way,
the truth, and the life. No one comes
to the Father except through Me."

John 14:6 NKJV

What are you offering up to the Lord? Is
it your praise and thanksgiving? Is it your
love and generosity? Your surrender and
obeys? What are you offering up today?

Start with thankfulness and praise, and
watch how He will guide your days.

Choose to live free. Choose to be an
example. Choose to be His hands and
feet. Do not live in the bondage of sin
because He gives us free will to choose.
Sin will only lead to death. Live free in

Him. Be guided and trust the Holy Spirit in you. Be free. Live as a child of the most high God and proclaim He has set you free today.

"As God's loving servants, you should live in complete freedom, but never use your freedom as a cover-up for evil."

1 Peter 2:16 TPT

Trust God with the impossible. Trust God with the wayward child. Trust God with your financial stresses and worries. Trust God with your spouse's health. Trust God for that friend that has lost their way. Trust God, oh, trust Him today. That's our hope, that's our faith.

Hope is what gets us through. Hope is our trust; you will pull through. We hope for a healing a miracle, a new way. We hope for You to come take our pain away. We hope for the future to be bright and great. We hope for the easy way. We hope, that's all we have. We hope to be glad and not feel sad. We hope trials never come. We hope at every beginning and in the middle some. With all this hope, the greatest Treasure we have is the very hope You will come back one day.

One with each other, one with You. Oh, our hearts long to be one. One accord. One church. One in love. One in truth. One seeing You. One, oh one, how You want us to become all one. I know this has to be Your heart, so why can't we all just be one?

I pray a unity of one in the last days to all come together and see it's one way.

As in heaven, we will live one day as one, oh, that's my faith.

ABOUT THE
Authors

*B*renda and Lacey are a dynamic mother daughter duo. They love Jesus above all. Brenda and her faith encourages her daughter to believe and dream. Lacey's passion for Jesus and writing blesses her mother to keep dreaming even bigger. They both are part of True Love Ministries in Bourbon, MO. They enjoy spending time together laughing and praying

www.ingramcontent.com/pod-product-compliance
Lightning Source LLC
Chambersburg PA
CBHW070453130626
46553CB00006B/2395